MW01253816

APPETIZERS
43 RECIPES

Nobu Kawakami

OVERSEAS DISTRIBUTORS

UNITED STATES: JP TRADING, INC.
                300 Industrial Way
                Brisbane, CA. 94005
                Phone: (415) 468-0775, 0776

MEXICO: Editorial Sayrols, S.A. de C.V.

COLOMBIA: Jorge E. Morales & CIA. LTDA.

TAIWAN: Formosan Magazine Press, Ltd.

HONG KONG: Apollo Book Company, Ltd.

THAILAND: Central Books Distribution Co., Ltd.

SINGAPORE: MPH DISTRIBUTORS (S) PTE, LTD.

MALAYSIA: MPH DISTRIBUTORS SDN. BHD.

PHILIPPINES: National Book Store, Inc.

KOREA: Tongjin Chulpan Muyeok Co., Ltd.

INDONESIA: C.V. TOKO BUKU "MENTENG"

INDIA: Dani Book Land, Bombay 14

AUSTRALIA: BOOKWISE INTERNATIONAL

GUAM, SIPAN AND MICRONESIAN ISLANDS: Fujiwara's Sales and Service

CANADA: MILESTONE PUBLICATIONS

U.S.A.: MASA T. & ASSOCIATES
       : A.K. HARANO COMPANY
       : D & BH ENTERPRISES

Original Copyright © 1997 by Nobu Kawakami

World rights reserved. Published by JOIE, INC. 1-8-3, Hirakawa-cho, Chiyoda-ku, Tokyo 102 Japan   Printed in Hong Kong

No part of this book or portions thereof may be reproduced in any form or by any means including electronic retrieval system without prior written approval from the author or publisher.

ISBN4-915831-77-9

ACKNOWLEDGMENTS

I would like to express my sincere gratitude to my publisher, Mr Shiro Shimura, who encouraged me to write this book. I am also grateful to Mr. and Mrs. Le Quillec, whose advice on the recipes was so helpful. Lastly to my assistants, I say "thank you" for all the efforts in producing the book.

Shiro Shimura, publisher, JOIE, INC.
Yoichi Matsuda, photographer
Mariko Suzuki, illustrator
Yoko Ishiguro, translator
Akira Naito, chief-editor
Koji Abe, Mieko Baba, editors

Nobu Kawakami

PREFACE

Recently, my gourmet friend, Mr. Shiro Shimura, the publisher, gave me a souvenir. It was a menu card from the kitchen I had trained in thirty-five years ago at Hotel George Cinq, in Paris. This single card encouraged me to start a new cookbook.

In this book you will find practical, easy-to-prepare dishes that can be served not only as appetizers, but as snacks for tea or lunch. I especially hope you will try the recipes that fuse French and Japanese flavors.

Dishes cooked with love and care will result in delightful tastes and bring smiles to the faces of your guests. I wrote this book with this simple motto in mind, and it is my sincere wish that the readers receive the same pleasures I continue to acquire from cooking.

Nobu Kawakami

July 1997
Tokyo

CONTENTS

USEFUL FACTS AND FIGURES

Remember: Japanese standard cup holds 200ml while the American cup is 240ml. The Japanese standard tablespoon (tbsp) holds 15ml and the teaspoon (tsp) 5ml as in most countries.

A 500 watt(w) microwave oven is used for the recipes. Some adjustments of the cooking time may be necessary depending on the power of your oven.

COLD APPETIZERS

Prosciutto Canapés
(See page 10)

Caviar Canapés
(See page 12)

Sea Urchin Roe Canapés
(See page 9)

Smoked Salmon Canapés
(See page 11)

Chevre Cheese Canapés
(See page 13)

Canapés
à la
Carte

Prepare Toast Squares

1 Trim away crusts from slices of bread.

2 Cut into quarters.

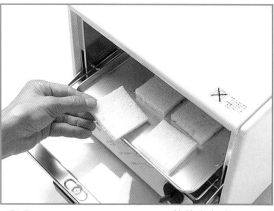

3 In a toaster oven, toast until lightly browned.

4 Spread butter sparingly on each slice.

Prepare Toast Rounds

1 Using a round, scalloped-edge cutter, cut out 4 rounds from each slice.

2 In a toaster oven, toast until lightly browned.

3 Spread butter sparingly on each slice.

Sea Urchin Roe Canapés

Ingredients: Makes 4

1 thin slice white bread
2 tbsps salted sea urchin roe
3 tbsps unsalted butter
Walnuts, crushed
Butter for spreading

Directions

1 Make square crusts referring to page 8.

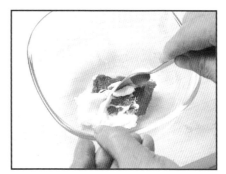

2 In a small bowl, combine sea urchin roe and unsalted butter. This is to decrease the saltiness of the sea urchin roe.

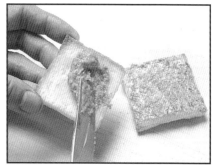

3 Spread the paste over each toast.

4 Scatter crushed walnuts, and press lightly to settle into the paste.

Prosciutto Canapés

Ingredients: Makes 4

1   thin slice white bread
2-3 thin slices prosciutto
2-3 cheese slices
½   small dill pickle
Butter for spreading

Directions

1 Make toast squares by referring to page 8.

2 Cut sliced cheese the same size as the toast, then into halves.

3 Place a piece of cheese on a piece of toast.

4 Cut prosciutto slightly larger than the toast, then into halves.

5 Place onto the toast, overlapping the cheese at center.

6 Slice dill pickle thinly.

7 Place in the center of canapé.

Smoked Salmon Canapés

Ingredients: Makes 4

1   thin slice white bread
2-3   slices smoked salmon
4   capers
Butter for spreading

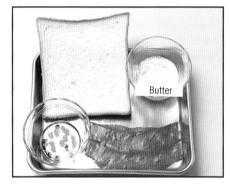

Directions

1 Make toast squares by referring to page 8.

2 Cut smoked salmon into the same size as the toast.

3 Place squarely on the toast.

4 Center a caper and press lightly to secure.

Caviar Canapés

Ingredients: Makes 4

1 thin slice white bread
2 tsps caviar
1 slice lemon
Butter for spreading

Directions

1 Make 4 toast rounds by referring to page 8.

2 Cut the lemon slice into thin sections.

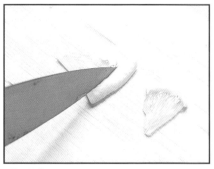

3 Trim away the rind.

4 Spread caviar onto toast.

5 Place a lemon triangle in the center.

Chevre Cheese Canapés

Ingredients: Makes 4

1   thin slice white bread
1½ oz (50g)   chevre cheese
    (Chevre cheese is a goat cheese, but
    can be substituted with plain natural
    cheese.)
I tbsp fresh cream
2   green olives
Mustard
1   sprig fresh thyme
Dash pepper
Butter for spreading

Directions

1 Make 4 toast rounds by referring to page 8.

2 Scrape white mold off cheese using the blade of a knife.

3 In a small bowl, soften the cheese with a fork.

4 Add fresh cream and mix until well blended.

5 Remove pits from olives.

6 Mince olives finely.

7 Add minced olives, crumbled thyme leaves and pepper into the cheese mixture.

8 Spoon into a piping bag fitted with a star nozzle and pipe onto the toast in a circle. Decorate with a thin slice of pitted olive, dill pickle or capers, if desired.

Decorated Deviled Eggs

Ham-and-Mint Deviled Eggs
(See page 21)

Olive Deviled Eggs
(See page 20)

Radish Deviled Eggs
(See Page 19)

Avocado Deviled Eggs
(See page 18)

Salmon Roe Deviled Eggs
(See Page 17)

How to cook hard-boiled eggs:

Place eggs in a saucepan and add enough cold water to cover. Heat until the temperature reaches 100 °F (40°C), turning the eggs occasionally so the egg yolks will be in the center. Bring to a boil and cook about 10 minutes; transfer to cold water and let stand until cool.

How to prepare mayonnaise or mustard deviled eggs

Take out yolks

1 Cut a hard-boiled egg lengthwise into halves, gently holding the egg in your palm. Cutting on a chopping board may squash the egg yolk and/or white.

2 Using a spoon, take out the yolk. Sprinkle the egg white with salt and pepper, if preferred.

3 Using a fork, mash the yolk.

Mayonnaise deviled egg

1 Add mayonnaise and ketchup to the mashed yolk; stir until well blended.

2 Using two spoons, fill the white with mayonnaise filling.

3 Shape the filling into a mound with the back of spoon.

Mustard deviled egg

1 Add softened butter and mustard to the mashed yolk; stir until well blended.

2 Using two spoons, fill the white with mustard filling.

3 Shape the filling into a mound with the back of spoon.

Salmon Roe Deviled Eggs

Ingredients: Makes 4

2	hard-boiled eggs
1½	tbsps butter
½	tsp mustard
1½	tbsps salted salmon roe
1-2	string beans
Pinch salt	

Directions

1 Make mustard deviled eggs by referring to page 16.

2 Bring salted water to a boil and briefly cook string beans.

3 Cut string beans into thin, diagonal slices.

4 Place salted salmon roe on the mustard deviled egg.

5 Decorate the egg with a string bean fan so it resembles a pineapple.

Avocado Deviled Eggs

Ingredients: Makes 4

2	hard-boiled eggs
2	tbsps mayonnaise
1	tsp tomato ketchup
½	medium avocado

Dash *akame* leaf buds
Few drops lemon juice

Directions

1 Make mayonnaise deviled eggs by referring to page 16.

2 Hold avocado stem end towards you, insert knife until it hits the pit.

3 Turn avocado, cutting around the pit.

4 Twist to separate the halves.

5 Strike the pit with the knife so it holds fast (not to damage the pulp).

6 Twist the pit with the knife to left and right.

7 Lift out the pit, and sprinkle the flesh with few drops of lemon juice to retain the color.

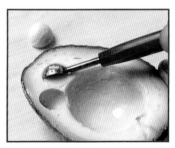

8 Use a melon baller to scoop out avocado flesh, or cut into cubes.

9 Place avocado balls on mayonnaise deviled egg.

10 Fill the center with *akame* leaf buds,(or tips of water cress).

✦ **Melon baller** ✦

Scoops out perfect balls of melon and other fruit. Use one to make vegetable balls, as well.

Radish Deviled Eggs

Ingredients: Makes 4

2   hard-boiled eggs
2   tbsps mayonnaise
1   tsp tomato ketchup
4   small radishes

Mayonnaise

Tomato ketchup

Directions

1 Make mayonnaise deviled eggs by referring to page 16.

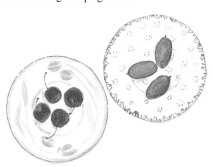

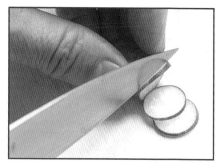

2 Slice radishes thinly.

3 Arrange radish slices in the filling to resemble flower petals. Place a dab of filling in center.

Olive Deviled Eggs

Ingredients: Makes 4

2	hard-boiled eggs
1½	tbsps butter
Mustard	
4	black olives
2	anchovy fillets

Directions

1 Make mustard deviled eggs by referring to page 16.

2 Remove pits from black olives.

3 Split anchovy fillets.

4 Roll half a fillet of anchovy around an olive.

5 Place on the mustard deviled egg.

Pitter

A pitter will remove the pits from cherries and olives quickly and easily without changing the round shape of the fruit.

Ham and Mint Deviled Eggs

Ingredients: Makes 4

2 hard-boiled eggs
1½ tbsps butter
Mustard
1 thin slice of ham
4 mint leaves

Directions

1 Make mustard deviled eggs by referring to page 16.

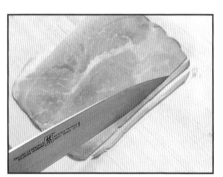

2 Cut a slice of ham into ⅛" (3mm) strips.

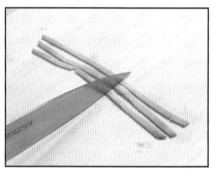

3 Cut the strips in half.

4 Place strips of ham on the mustard filling, forming a lattice.

5 Garnish with a mint leaf.

Fancy Eggs: Smoked Salmon

Ingredients: Makes 4

4	hard-boiled eggs	Lemon juice
8	thin slices smoked salmon	Dill sprigs
4	tbsps salted salmon roe	Anise seeds
1	tbsp fresh cream	Salt and pepper

22

Directions

1 Peel the boiled egg and cut off one end so the yolk can be removed.

2 Using a small spoon, scoop out the yolk.

3 Mash the yolk with a fork.

4 Mix in fresh cream.

5 Add lemon juice and blend well.

6 Cut 2 smoked salmon slices into ³/₄" (2cm) strips parallel to the flake lines.

7 Add salmon and anise seeds to the yolk mixture.

8 Season with salt and pepper.

9 Sprinkle the white with a pinch of salt and fill the hollow with the yolk mixture.

10 Lay 1.5 slices of smoked salmon over the side of an egg cup. Set the deviled egg an top add salmon roe and garnish with dill.

Tips

Create an elegant image. with this combination of orange colors and rich seafood.It will be a party favorite.

23

Ingredients: Makes 4

4	hard-boiled eggs	1	cucumber
½	large carrot		Salt to taste
½	small potato	1	tbsp mayonnaise
1	string bean		Lemon juice

Directions

1 Scoop out cooked yolks and mash them in the same manner as Fancy Eggs on page 22-23.

2 Cook string bean in salted boiling water.

3 Place potato half and ⅓ oz (10g) carrot in an ovenproof container, with cut edges down. Cover and coook in microwave oven (500w) about 2 minutes.

4 Dice cooked string bean, carrot and potato into ¼"(6mm) pieces.

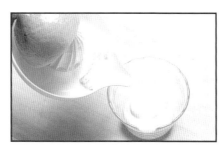

5 Mix mayonnaise and lemon juice.

6 Add mayonnaise mixture to the vegetables. Add mashed yolk and mix well.

7 Sprinkle egg white with a pinch of salt. Fill the hollow with the vegetable mixture forming a mound.

8 Cut carrot lengthwise into a very thin strip and boil in salted water.

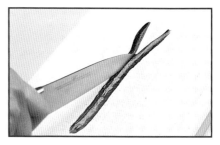

9 Peel cucumber and cut into very thin strips. Boil in salted water to soften.

10 Tie carrot and cucumber strips as shown and set onto the deviled egg.

Tips

Deviled eggs set in cute egg cups will inspire a pleasant conversation.

Tricolor Cheese Balls

Ingredients: Makes 4

7 oz (200g) leftover cheese
(any natural cheese of 2 or 3 different types)
1 tsp cognac
Walnuts
Curry powder
Paprika

A good way to use up leftover cheese. Any strong cheese can be blended into a mild tasting mixture.

Directions

1 In a bowl, place several kinds of cheese and mash with a fork.

2 Add cognac and mix well.

3 Stir until even and smooth.

4 Using two spoons, take a small amount and shape into ½ "(1.5cm) ball. Make 12.

Walnut cheese balls

5 Chop walnuts.

6 Put chopped walnuts and cheese ball in a small plastic bag. Gently shake the bag until the cheese is completely covered with walnut.

Curry cheese balls

7 In another small plastic bag put curry powder and add cheese ball. Gently shake the bag until the cheese is completely covered with curry powder.

Paprika cheese balls

8 In another small plastic bag put paprika and add cheese ball. Gently shake the bag until the cheese is completely covered with paprika.

Tips

Cheese ball are fun and easy to pick up if displayed in paper cups. Serve with French bread or crackers.

Paprika cheese balls

Walnut cheese balls

Curry cheese balls

Ingredients: Serves 2

1 small calamari
1/2 stalk thick celery
Lemon balm

Sauce:
3 1/2 tbsps mayonnaise
1 1/2 tbsps fresh cream
1/2 tbsp fresh ginger juice

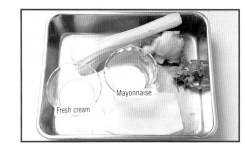

Directions

1 Skin calamari, if not peeled, and cut into 1/8" (3mm) strips.

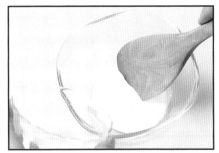

2 In a bowl, combine mayonnaise, fresh cream and ginger juice.

3 Remove celery strings.

4 Cut celery into 1 1/2" (4cm) lengths and flatten with your palm.

5 Cut celery horizontally into 4 thin slices.

6 Stack all celery slices and shred into matchsticks.

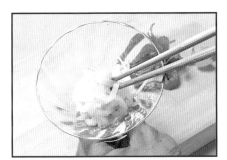

7 Place calamari in a serving glass, drizzle on the sauce and garnish with lemon balm sprigs.

Tips

Calamari usually has skin on both sides. Peeling the tough outer skin takes a little patience, but the taste is worth the effort.

Flounder Cocktail

This dish brings out the natural sweetness of the fresh fish, with an accent of herb in the sour cream sauce.

Ingredients: Serves 2

½ fillet fresh flounder
½ cucumber
Pinch salt
8 leaves Boston lettuce

Sauce
1 large *shiso* leaf (perilla)
1½ tbsps fresh cream
3½ tbsps sour cream
Pinch salt

Directions

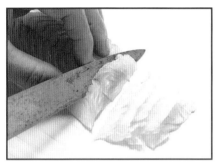

1 Cut flounder fillet diagonally into thin slices.

2 In a small bowl, combine fresh cream and sour cream. Season with salt and mix in shredded *shiso* leaf.

3 Rub the cucumber skin with salt; wash and drain. (Salt brings out a fresh green color of cucumber and also soften the tough skin.)

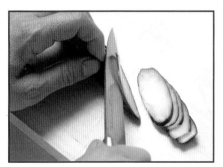

4 Cut cucumber diagonally into thin slices. (This way each strip will have green skin on both ends)

5 Stagger the slices and cut into fine strips.

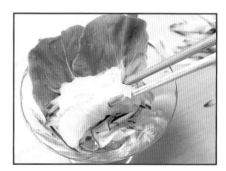

6 Line a serving glass with lettuce leaves. Lay in cucumber strips and place flounder on top. Drizzle on the cream sauce..

Tips

Prepare this in large amount and serve it as *sashimi* salad.

Camembert and Apple Slices

Ingredients: Serves 4

1   package (4 1/2 oz, 125g) camembert cheese
1   tart apple
Lemon juice

Directions

1 Cut camembert cheese equally into 8.

2 Cut apple into halves and cut each half into 3.

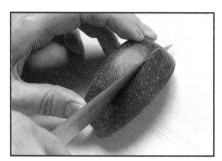

3 Cut each wedge into halves again.

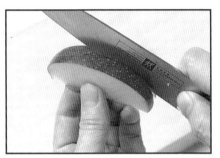

4 Score each wedge lengthwise 1/3 of the way from the edge.

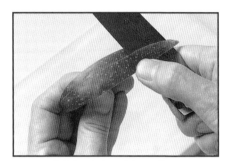

5 Peel 2/3 of the skin off. Make 6 of these ribboned apple slices.

6 Peel remaining apple slices completely.

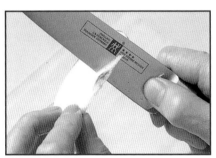

7 Remove the core. Put slices into a small bowl.

8 Sprinkle apple slices with lemon juice to prevent discoloration.

9 Tilt the bowl several times so the apples absorb the lemon juice.

Tips

Serve cheese at room temperature.

Choufleur à la Grece

Ingredients: Serves 4

17 oz (500g) cauliflower
1   clove garlic
1   cup olive oil
1   cup white wine
1   tbsp lemon juice
1   bay leaf
1   tsp coriander
1   tsp salt
1   tsp white peppercorn

White peppercorn
White wine
Olive oil
Salt
Coriander

Directions

1 Separate cauliflower into florets.

2 Cut each floret into bite-size pieces.

3 Peel the garlic.

4 In a saucepan, heat 1½ tbsps olive oil and lightly fry the cauliflower and the whole garlic clove.

5 Add white wine, lemon juice and remaining olive oil.

6 Add bay leaf and coriander seeds.

7 Season with salt and add white peppercorn.

8 Cover with a circle of parchment and cook about 10 minutes. Do not use aluminum foil as the acidity may draw out the aluminum.

9 When a bamboo skewer can be inserted easily (do not overcook), remove from heat and let stand to cool.

Tips

Keep in an air-tight jar for later use. Try with celery, broccoli or cucumber, but not with tender vegetables.

Marinated Eel

Ingredients: 4-6 servings

2   steamed small eels
1   shallot
2   small sweet pickles
2   tbsps white wine
Salt and pepper to taste

Eel is often stewed in red wine, but this is a delightfully different new treat.

Directions

1 Make deep incisions into shallot, leaving the root end to hold together.

2 Make deep incisions crosswise this time into thickness.

3 Mince finely.

4 Cut sweet pickle lengthwise into quarters.

5 Cut into small pieces.

6 Cut eel into bite-size pieces and sprinkle with salt and pepper.

7 In a glass casserole, lay the cut eel and scatter with minced shallots.

8 Scatter on pickles.

9 Sprinkle with white wine and let stand I hour, then turn over and marinate another hour.

10 Cover with plastic wrap making sure not to touch the eel. Microwave about 1 minute in 500w oven.

Tips

Pungent aroma of shallots and pickles excites your appetite. Serve hot or cold, with a serving spoon.

Carrot Salad

Ingredients: Serves 4

2 medium carrots (10 oz, 300g)

Vinaigrette
$^1/_4$ cup (50ml) vinegar
$^3/_4$ cup (150ml) vegetable oil
1 tsp salt
Dash pepper

Salt
Pepper
Vegetable oil
Vinegar

Vinaigrette

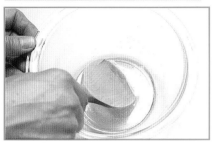

1 In a bowl, mix vinegar, salt and pepper until the salt is completely dissolved.

2 Add oil and blend well.

✦ Rotary vegetable grater ✦

This easy to use grater makes rough edges on grated vegetables which absorb dressings well.

Directions

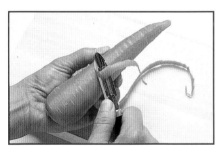

1 Wash and peel carrots.

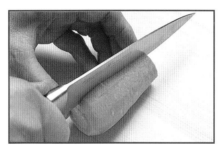

2 Cut in half, then again in half lengthwise.

3 Cut again in half. If using small carrots, cut into quarters lengthwise.

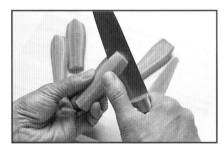

4 Cut off the cores.

5 Cut into 1 1/2 "(4cm) lengths.

6 Put the carrots in a rotary grater and grate. Mix with vinaigrette.

Tips

Can be marinated for 2-3 days so the sauce will be well absorbed. Keeps indefinitely if refrigerated.

Red Cabbage and Lettuce Salad

Ingredients: Serves 4

½ head red cabbage
Salt and vinegar
½ head iceberg lettuce
Vinaigrette
  2 tbsps vinegar
  6 tbsps vegetable oil
Salt and pepper to taste
(See page 39 for directions)

Red cabbage should be boiled first as it is very tough when fresh. Pour vinegar over it while hot, and it will turn a beautiful fuchsia.

Directions

1 Cut a half head of red cabbage in half.

2 Remove the core.

3 Remove hard stems. (Use them in soups)

4 Cut into ⅛"(3mm) strips.

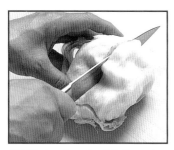

5 Cut a head of lettuce in half.

6 Cut one half into ¼" (6mm) strips.

7 In boiling salted water, cook red cabbage until crisptender, about 2 minutes. Do not overcook since the color will fade.

8 Drain and put back into the hot saucepan.

9 Sprinkle with vinegar while hot and mix well. Let stand to cool.

10 Drain off vinegar and mix with half of the vinaigrette.

11 Just before serving, mix lettuce with remaining dressing.

Tips

Arrange nicely in a serving dish to show the contrasting colors.

41

Leek Rolls

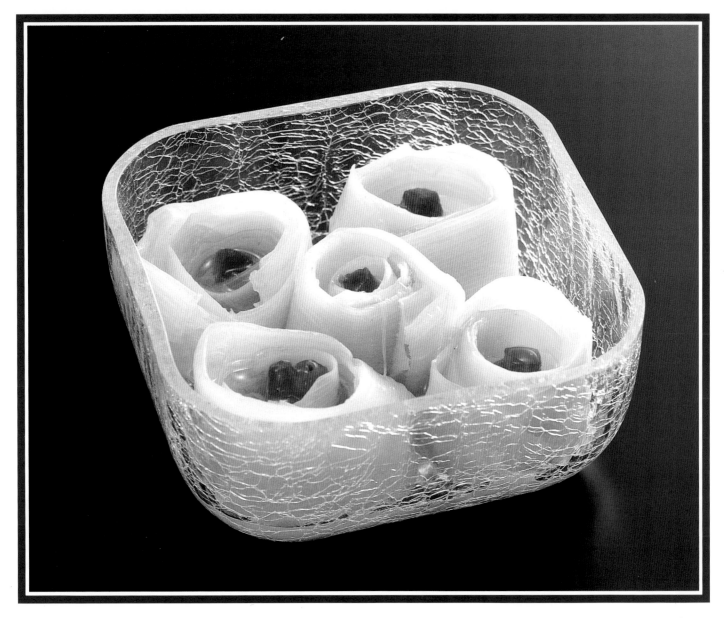

Ingredients: Serves 4

2   small leeks
Pinch salt
1   tomato, diced in ½ "(6mm)
Vinaigrette
  1   tbsps vinegar
  3   tbsps vegetable oil
  Salt and pepper to taste
  (See page 39 for directions)

Pepper

Salt

Vegetable oil   Vinegar

Directions

Or lay the leek on a chopping board, green ends towards you, and pull the knife as shown.

1 Insert a knife, blade edge up, into the green part of leek.

2 Make criss-cross incisions to quarter the green part.

3 Wash under running water separating each layer. (Be sure to remove the dirt in the center)

4 Cook in boiling salted water until tender, 12-15 minutes. (If cooking large amount, bind with thread)

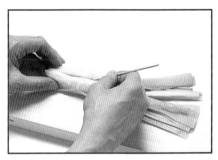

5 Using a sharp-pointed skewer, tear leek lengthwise in half. (This way the straight tissues are not damaged)

6 Cut in half, if necessary, into 6"(15cm) lengths.

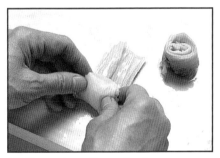

7 Loosely roll up the layers.

8 Decorate with diced tomato and pour vinaigrette over the top.

Endive and Bell Pepper Salad

Ingredients: Serves 4

2   heads endive
¹/₄   each red, yellow and green bell pepper
2²/₃ oz (80g) gruyere cheese
Vinaigrette
  2 tbsps vinegar
  3 tbsps vegetable oil
  Salt and pepper to taste
  (See page 39 for directions)
Walnuts, crushed

Thick flesh of bell peppers teams well with endive both in texture and color. The key to tender peppers is to peel them.

Directions

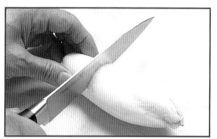

1 Wash endives well. Cut off root ends to fit the serving dish.

2 Cut the root ends into $3/8$"(1cm) width.

3 Cut gruyere cheese into $3/8$" (1cm) cubes.

4 Peel bell peppers using a parer.

5 Trim away the stems and seeds.

6 Cut in half crosswise.

7 Shred into $1/8$"(3mm) strips. Prepare 2 other peppers the same.

8 Create a flower with endive leaves.

9 Combine endive, peppers and cheese. Place on the endive leaves.

10 Scatter crushed walnuts and serve with vinaigrette.

Tips

Mix with vinaigrette just before serving each salad. Serve with a spoon and fork.

✦ Vegetable parer ✦

An essential utensil in the kitchen for peeling fruits and vegetables. Choose one that fits your hand.

Radish Bites

Ingredients: Serves 4

25-30 radishes
Butter
Salt

Radishes which originated in China are said to have been eaten for three thousand years. They have even been discovered fossilized in the pyramids of Egypt. Enjoy the natural taste , in a simple but delicious way.

Directions

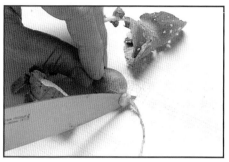

1 Wash radishes carefully. Discard roots and large leaves.

2 Arrange nicely on a serving plate, and serve with butter and table knives. Sprinkle with salt, if desired. Accompany with buttered toast.

Tips

Butter can be sandwiched between thin slices of radish and arranged on a plate, if you prefer.

Eating suggestions

1 Using a table knife, make an incision into the center of a radish.

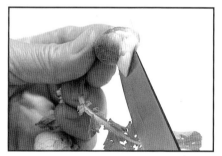

2 Insert a dab of butter into the incision.

Roquefort Pastry Sticks

Ingredients: Serves 4-6

2 sheets (7" × 7", 18cm × 18cm each)
frozen puff pastry
1 oz (30g) roquefort cheese
1 egg, beaten

Directions

1 Preheat the oven to 425 °F (220°C). Slice roquefort cheese thinly.

2 Roll out a thawed pastry sheet thin.

3 Roll out in the other direction. Prepare 2 sheets the same size.

4 Scatter roquefort cheese evenly on one pastry sheet.

5 Overlay plastic wrap and roll out cheese until thin.

6 Remove the plastic wrap and overlay another pastry sheet.

7 Using a pastry divider, cut in half.

8 Brush on some water over one half.

9 Lay the other half on top. Roll out into 1/8" (3mm) thickness. Cover and refrigerate at least 1 hour.

10 Cut into 3/8"(1cm) strips.

11 Wet your fingers with water and sprinkle over a baking dish. This is to prevent the pastry sticks from rolling over.

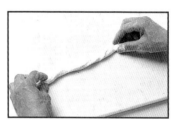

12 On a flat surface, twist the pastry strips.

13 Place on the baking dish and brush with beaten egg. (The water on the baking dish keeps the sticks still)

14 Bake about 10 minutes until crisp. Cut in half crosswise while hot. (The pastry will smash if cut cold)

Tips

Arrange on a tray lined with a lace doily.

49

Miniature Cheese Puffs

Ingredients: Makes 30

2   oz (60g) unsalted butter
³⁄₅ cup (120ml) water
¹⁄₂ tbsp granulated sugar
3   oz (90g) plain flour
2   eggs, beaten
¹⁄₃ oz (10g) gruyere cheese
Pinch salt

Directions

1 Preheat oven to 350°F (180°C), In a saucepan, heat water, sugar, salt and butter until bubbly.

2 Remove from heat and add flour all at once. Beat with a wooden spatula.

3 Continue beating until it is smooth and easily pulls away from the sides of the pan forming a ball.

4 Return to heat and stir to release extra moisture. Keep stirring until the bottom of the pan has little white scorch mark.

5 Remove from heat and cool slightly. Add beaten eggs, a little at a time, beating after each addition.

6 Beat vigorously and thoroughly. This procedure is very important to make fluffy puffs.

7 Check the consistency by raising the spatula to see if the dough falls slowly.

8 Using a rubber spatula, put the dough into a piping bag with a plain, 3/8" (1cm) nozzle.

9 Pipe 3/4" (2cm) diam. mounds onto the baking dish.

10 Brush the surfaces with beaten eggs.

11 Using a wet fork, press the surfaces to make criss-cross marks.

12 Grate gruyere cheese.

13 Using a spoon, top the pastry mounds with grated cheese. Bake at 350°F(175°C) about 16 minutes. The bottoms will be flat if successful.

Tips

Pile up in a tray lined with lace doily or napkin.

⁜ Cheese grater ⁜

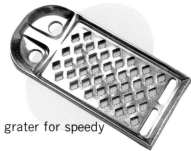

Choose a sharp edged grater for speedy grating.

HOT APPETIZERS

Prunes in Bacon

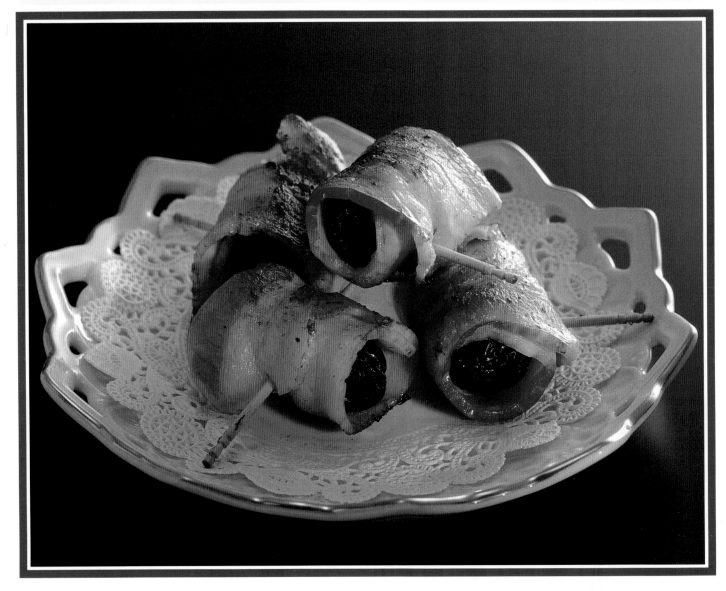

Ingredients: Serves 4

12 prunes
4 strips bacon
Vegetable oil for frying

Pork teams well with sweet and tart food, hence this combination.

Directions

1 Cut into a prune until the knife touches the stone.

2 Remove the stone. Pit the remaining prunes.

3 Chop 4 prunes to stuff the other prunes.

4 Shape the whole prune pulling the skin smooth.

5 Stuff the whole prunes with chopped prunes.

6 Cut bacon strips in half. Wrap the stuffed prune with the bacon.

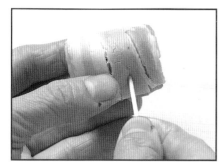

7 Secure the end with a toothpick. Make 8 rolls.

8 In a preheated frying pan, heat a little salad oil and fry the bacon rolls. Turn over and cook the other side.

Tips

How about serving with choice aperitifs?

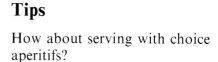

Bananas in Ham

Ingredients: Makes 2

1   banana
Dash lemon juice
4   thin slices ham
Green peppercorn
2   tbsps butter

Green peppercorn   Butter

Cooked bananas taste entirely different from raw ones. Green peppercorns accent the taste.

Directions

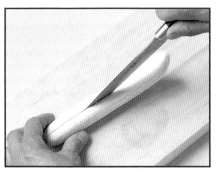

1 Peel banana and cut lengthwise in half.

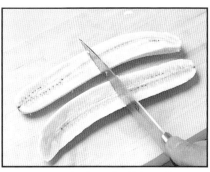

2 Cut again into half lengths.

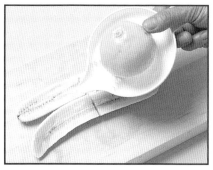

3 Sprinkle with lemon juice to prevent discoloring.

4 Scatter green peppercorns over a slice of ham. Do not place peppercorns on far end since they roll out.

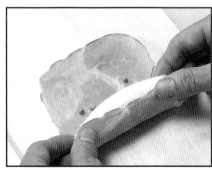

5 Add a piece of banana and wrap with ham; secure the end with a toothpick.

6 Grease an oven proof serving plate with butter.

7 Place rolled ham and brush melted butter over the top.

8 Microwave uncovered, about 2 minutes in a 500w oven.

Tips

Remove the toothpicks before serving. The rolls can be cut into small pieces. Serve hot or cold.

Pigs in Blankets

Ingredients: Serves 4

1   sheet (7" × 7", 18cm × 18cm) frozen puff pastry
8   cocktail frankfurters
1   egg, beaten

Extra easy sausage cocktails made in a jiffy.

1 Preheat oven to 425 °F(220°C). Cut thawed puff pastry into 4 strips.

2 Cut in half lengthwise to make 8 strips.

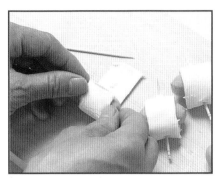

3 Using a fork or toothpick, prick the frankfurters to prevent the skin from tearing. Wrap with pastry strips.

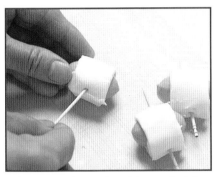

4 Secure the ends with toothpicks.

5 To prevent the rolls from moving in the next step, wet your hand and sprinkle over the baking dish.

6 Put pastry rolls on the baking dish and brush with beaten egg.

7 Apply another coat of beaten egg and bake about 10 minutes until golden and puffy.

Tips

Do not remove the toothpicks as they work as handles. Serve hot.

Calamari in Herb Butter Sauce

Ingredients: Serves 4

1   fresh calamari
2-3 sprigs parsley
2" (5cm) green onion
2   cloves garlic
1   tbsp white wine
2⅔ oz (80g) butter
Dash pepper

A special treat featuring a herbal sauce over calamari.

Directions

1 Mince parsley leaves. Make lengthwise cuts into green onion at several angles.

2 Finely mince green onion.

3 Peel garlic cloves and make several cuts parallel to the grain.

4 Mince finely.

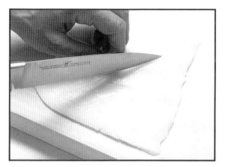

5 Peel the skin of calamari and score outside surface in a diamond pattern.

6 Cut lengthwise in half and then into ³/₄ "(2cm) strips.

7 In a small bowl, mix garlic, green onion, parsley and softened butter (save ¹/₃ oz, 10g for frying). Sprinkle with pepper and wine; mix well.

8 In a frying pan, melt the remaining ¹/₃ oz (10g) butter and fry the calamari strips over high heat.

9 Add herb butter and coat the calamari; immediately transfer to a serving plate.

Tips

Serve with French bread to dip in the savory sauce.

Deep-fried Camembert Triangles

Ingredients: Serves 4

1   package (4²/₃ oz,125g) camembert cheese
1   egg, beaten
Bread crumbs
Vegetable oil for deep-frying

An unbeatable favorite the combination of crisp outside and rich, creamy camembert inside is always enjoyable.

Directions

1 Lightly scrape the white mold off the cheese so the beaten egg will stick well.

2 Cut camembert cheese into 8 triangles.

3 Coat each triangle with beaten egg.

4 Coat with bread crumbs.

5 Dip in beaten egg again to coat the whole surface.

6 Coat again with bread crumbs.

7 Heat oil very hot so bread crumbs dropped on the surface sizzle at once.

8 Deep-fry cheese about 1.5-2 minutes, occasionally turning for an even color.

9 Remove from oil when golden brown.

Tips
Serve with Boston lettuce leaves and endive, if desired.

Green Asparagus with Sauce Mousseline

Ingredients: Serves 4

12 stalks fresh green asparagus
2 egg yolks
$1/4$ cup water
$3^1/2$ oz (100g) unsalted butter
$2/3$ tbsp fresh cream
Salt and pepper

Water   Pepper   Salt   Butter   Fresh cream   Egg yolk

This rich but light whipped sauce complements the taste of green asparagus.

Directions

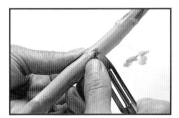

1 Using a vegetable parer, scrape hard spears.

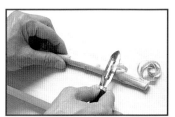

2 Lay asparagus on a chopping board and peel from the middle towards root end, leaving ³/₈"(1cm) unpeeled.

3 Cut off the root end with the peels attached, ½" (1.5cm) from the end. This way you can discard the peels and stem at one time. Prepare all asparagus.

4 Bunch asparagus to prevent the spears from breaking while in boiling water. (Also, it makes lifting from water easies)

5 In boiling salted water, cook asparagus until tender.

6 Take out asparagus and drain. Unbind and wrap in a clean napkin to keep warm.

7 In a small saucepan or double-boiler, combine egg yolks, salt, pepper and water.

8 Beat the mixture over a 125°F (50°C) water bath.

9 Beat until thick.

10 Stir in butter, a small cube at a time, beating after each addition.

11 When the butter is blended, stir in fresh cream.

Tips
Serve wrapped in a cloth, with sauce mouseline and a knife.

Eating suggestions
Cut asparagus and dip in the sauce.

Separating an egg
Break the egg shell in the middle and drain off white, transferring the yolk into each shell.

Tofu Gratin

Healthy and nutritious tofu grilled in foil.

Ingredients: Serves 4

1   cake firm *tofu*
4   slices (2", 5cm square each) gruyere cheese
2   slices lean sausage
Parsley
1   tbsp butter
1   tbsp tomato ketchup
1   tbsp Worcestershire sauce
Salt and pepper

Directions

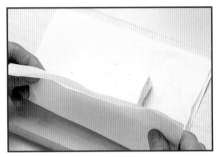

1 Wrap *tofu* in paper towel.

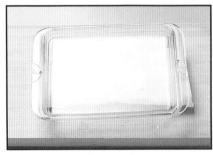

2 Put on a flat surface and press with a weight such as a casserole and drain off water about 1 hour.

If using a dehydrating film, no weight is necessary.

The film will absorb the moisture in 30 minutes.

3 Cut *tofu* into quarters and then into half thicknesses.

4 Grease the center of aluminum foil with butter.

5 Place drained *tofu* and sprinkle with salt and pepper.

6 Cut sausage slices into quarters.

7 Lay sausage pieces that are trimmed to fit the *tofu* on top.

8 Layer with another piece of *tofu* sprinkled with salt and pepper.

9 Layer again with sausage.

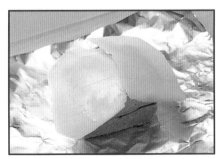

10 Top with gruyere cheese that is cut are larger than *tofu*.

11 Mince parsley.

12 Combine tomato ketchup and Worcestershire sauce.

13 Center the tofu on foil and top with sauce.

14 Place minced parsley on the sauce.

15 Wrap loosely, with aluminum foil Do not let the foil the surface.

16 Fold the edges to seal completely and grill in a toaster oven about 5 minutes until steaming hot. If making a large quantity, bake 15-20 minutes in a 400°F (200°C) oven.

Tips
Serve hot with a knife and fork to cut open the foil.

⊹ Cheese slicer ⊹

A very useful cooking tool to scrape a block of cheese into thin and even slices.

Avocado Gratin

Ingredients: Serves 4

2   avocados
4   large shrimp or 12 small shrimp
White wine
4   tbsps mayonnaise
Green onion
2   heaping tbsps grated gruyere cheese
Salt and pepper

Easy but flavorful cooked avocado.

Directions

1 Hold avocado stem end towards you, insert knife until it hits the pit.

2 Turn avocado, cutting around the pit.

3 Twist to separate the halves.

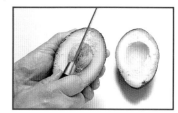

4 Strike the pit with the knife and twist the knife to left and right.

5 Lift out the pit.

6 Devein shrimp and sprinkle with salt and pepper.

7 In a saucepan bring white wine to a boil. Add shrimp and cook covered on high heat.

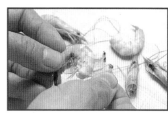

8 Shell shrimp.

9 Lightly holding the tail, pull out the flesh. This way you can shell the whole shrimp.

10 Chop shrimp coarsely.

11 Thinly slice green onion.

12 In a small bowl, combine shrimp, green onion, mayonnaise and pepper.

13 Fill the hollow of avocado with the mayonnaise mixture.

14 Top with cheese generously.

15 Microwave uncovered about 2 minutes.

16 Decorate cooked avocado with shrimp heads.

Tips

Serve hot with a spoon.

Croquer Monsieur

Ingredients: Makes 1

2 thin slices white bread
1 slice gruyere cheese
1 slice ham
2 tbsps butter

Hot and crisp sandwich with melting cheese inside is also good as a snack.

Directions

1 Spread butter on a surfaces of bread. For more crispness, toast before spreading.

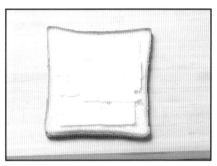

2 Lay cheese on the bread.

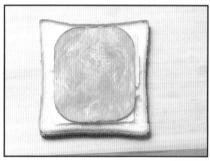

3 Lay a slice of ham on cheese.

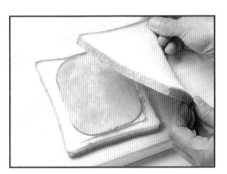

4 Top with another slice of buttered bread.

5 Spread butter generously over the top. Repeat on the other side. This is the key to a golden toast.

6 Melt butter in a frying pan.

7 Place the sandwich in the pan. Gently press down with a spatula.

8 Turn over when golden, and fry the other side.

Tips

Serve while the cheese is hot. For an appetizer, cut into small rounds with a cutter.

Harvest Moon Brioche

Ingredients: Serves 4

4   brioches
2   slices ham
4   small eggs
2   tbsps butter
Dash pepper

This brioche, stuffed with ham and egg can be served as an one dish breakfast.

Directions

1 Cut brioche near the top.

2 Insert a table knife at a point ³/₈ ”(1cm) from the bottom.

3 Push the knife deeper to loosen the bottom of hollow. Do not widen out the incision.

4 Cut into the top, ³/₈ ”(1cm) in from the outer edges all the way round.

5 Lift out the center.

6 Lightly spread butter over inside.

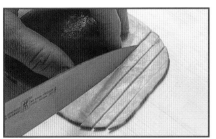

7 Cut ham into julienne strips.

8 Cut into ¹/₄ ”(6mm) squares.

9 Spoon ham into the hollow of brioche.

10 Pour in an egg, adjusting the amount of white to the size of hollow. Microwave about 30 seconds at 500w, uncovered.

11 Transfer into a toaster oven and cook until the yolk is half set. If cooked only with microwave oven, the egg will become tough.

Tips

Serve with a spoon and a salt shaker.

Quiche Lorraine

Ingredients: Makes 4 small (3½", 9cm) tarts

Shortcrust pastry
  2½ oz (750g) unsalted butter
  5   oz (150g) plain flour
  ¼   cup (50ml) cold wter
Pinch salt
Extra flour for rolling

Filling
  2 eggs
  ¾ cup (150ml) fresh cream
  ½ tsp salt
  Nutmeg
  ⅔ oz (20g) gruyere cheese
  1⅓ oz (40g) ham
  1⅓ oz (40g) bacon
  Dash pepper

Quiche Lorraine originated in Alsace, France. It is everyone's favorite today.

How to make shortcrust pastry for tartlets

1 In a food processor, put flour and cold butter cut into 1"(2cm) cubes.

2 Process just until the mixture resembles coarse bread crumbs.

3 Transfer to a bowl and make a hole in center. Add cold water.

4 Add salt.

5 Using chopsticks or a fork, mix lightly.

6 Using a pastry scraper, compress the mixture and divide into halves.

7 Lift one half with the scraper, and put on top of the other half.

8 Press down firmly.

9 Repeat the same procedure (step 6-8) 3-4 times until the surface is smooth.

10 Wrap in plastic wrap, smoothing the surface with a rolling pin.

11 Put in a plastic bag and refrigerate at least 2 hours.

12 Lightly flour the rolling surface.

13 Place the chilled dough and lightly flour it as well.

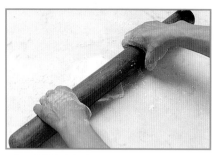

14 Divide into quarters, and roll out each piecce.

15 Roll into to a circle of about ¹/₈"(3mm) thickness.

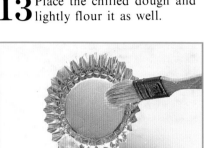

16 Grease the tartlet tin or aluminum pan with salad oil.

17 Lift the dough with the rolling pin.

18 Place the dough over the tin.

19 Fold the dough that falls outside so as to make thick sides.

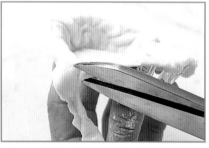

20 Trim away excess dough with scissors.

21 Shape the edges nicely with your fingers.

22 With floured fingers, press the sides to shape; refrigerate until chilled.

76

How to make egg mixture

1 Lightly beat eggs and add fresh cream.

2 Add salt and grated nutmeg.

3 Mix until well blended.

How to make Quiche Lorraine

1 Make a shortcrust pastry referring to page 75-76.

2 Make egg mixture as shown above.

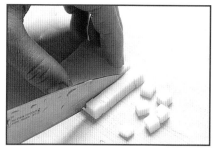

3 Reheat oven to 400°F (200°C). Dice gruyere cheese into 1/4" (6mm) cubes.

4 Dice bacon in the same manner as cheese and sprinkle with pepper.

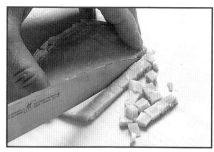

5 Dice ham in the same manner.

6 In a tin lined with shortcrust pastry add cheese, bacon and ham.

7 Pour in egg mixture. Bake about 15 minutes. Unmold and bake a further 5 minutes.

Tips
Petit Quiche Lorraine can be picked up by hand and eaten with a paper napkin at a party.

Leek Tartlets

Ingredients: Makes 4 small (3½", 9cm) tarts

Shortcrust pastry
  2½ oz (75g) unsalted butter
  5   oz (150g) plain flour
  ¼ cup (50ml) cold water
Pinch salt
Extra flour for rolling

Egg mixture
  2 eggs
  ¾ cup (150ml) fresh cream
  Pinch salt
  Dash nutmeg
  (See page 77 for directions)
¼ stalk (3 oz, 90g) leek
Salt and pepper
1 tbsp butter
1 cup (200ml) beer
1⅓ oz (40g) bacon

Savory tartlet with beer-braised leek. Make a variation with sauteed spinach.

Directions

1 Make a shortcrust pastry referring to page 75-76.

2 Make egg mixture referring to page 77.

3 Preheat oven to 400 °F (200°C). On a chopping board, cut into the green part of leek, lengthwise.

4 Make another cut the other way.

5 Cut into 1"(2.5cm) lengths and wash well.

6 Melt butter in a saucepan and release extra moisture. (Wait for a sizzling sound)

7 Fry the leek stirring constantly.

8 Season with salt and pepper.

9 Add beer.

10 Cover the surface with parchment and simmer until tender (about 15-20 minutes).

11 Transfer to a shallow container and let stand to cool.

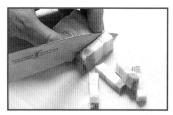

12 Cut bacon into 3/8" (1cm) sticks.

13 Add to a saucepan filled with water and bring to a boil.

14 Cook about 1 minute.

15 Drain off water and wash bacon under running water.

16 Line tartlet tin with shortcrust pastry and add bacon and leek.

17 Pour in egg mixture and bake about 15 minutes in oven. Unmold and bake a further 5 minutes.

APPETIZER COCKTAILS

Here are some of light, fruity cocktails to go with the appetizers.

Cocktail Kawakami

This refreshing cocktail was created by Cointreau S.A., France, in celebration of the Gold Medal given to me by the Mayor of Paris in 1985.
Enjoy the beautiful blend of Japanese *sake* and white curaçao liqueur.

Ratio of ingredients

3   parts *sake*, chilled
3   parts cointreau, chilled
4   parts grapefruit juice
A drop grenadine syrup

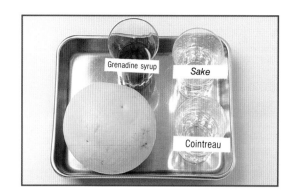

Directions

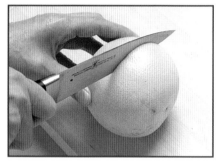

1 Cut grapefruit in half.

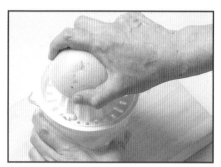

2 Squeeze with a juicer. Strain and chill juice.

3 In a chilled glass, add *sake* and cointreau.

4 Add grapefruit juice and mix well.

5 Add a drop of grenadine syrup to finish.

Tips

Stir well before serving.
If you make a large quantity in a jug, add grenadine syrup after pouring into individual glasses.

This is said to have been originated by a housewife who lived in Dijon, France, where cassis or red currants are abundant.

Ratio of ingredients

1   part crème de cassis
9   parts dry white wine, chilled

Cream de cassis

White wine

Directions

1 Pour crème de cassis into a chilled glass.

2 Pour in white wine and mix until well blended.

Noilly Framboise

Ratio of ingredients

1 part crème de framboise
9 parts dry Noilly Prat,
 or French dry vermouth

Cream de framboise

White wine

Directions

1 Pour crème de framboise into a glass.

2 Pour in Noilly Prat and stir well.

Tips

Noilly Prat can be substituted for a martini.

Kir Breton

Ratio of ingredients

1 part crème de cassis
9 parts dry cidre, chilled

Cream de cassis

Dry cidre

Directions

1 Pour crème de cassis into a glass.

2 Pour in cidre and stir well. Adjust the ratio to your tasts.